DIY FOR BOYS

READY, AIM, FIRE!

Marshmallow shooter

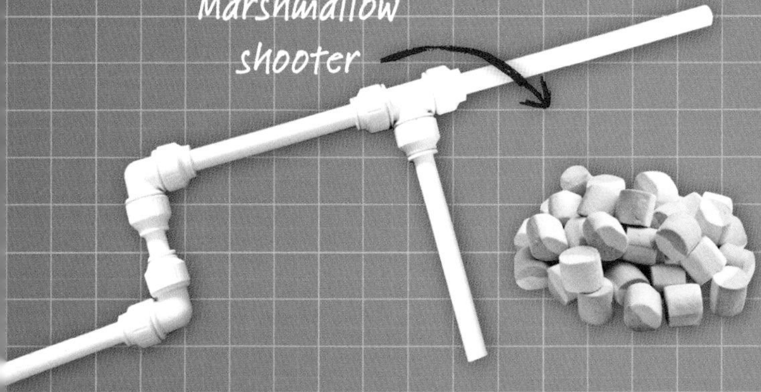

Mini wooden crossbow

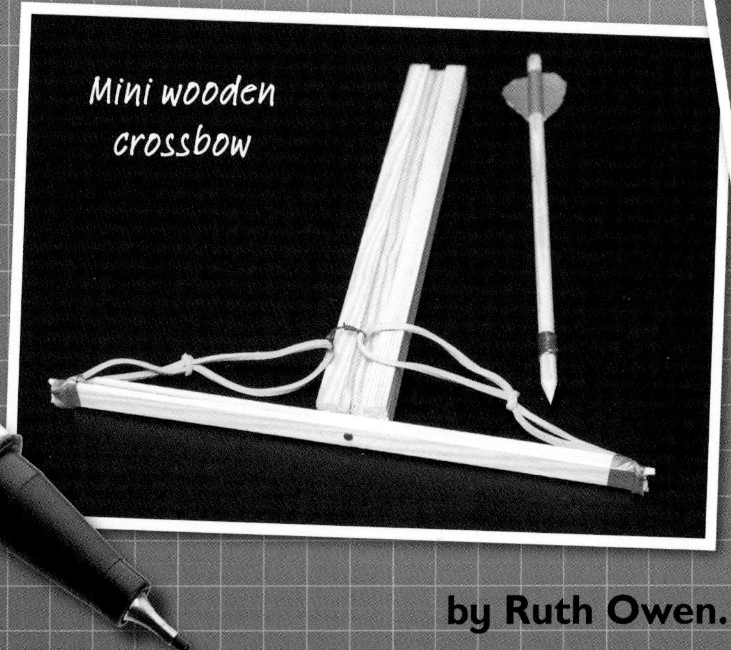

Bow and arrow

by Ruth Owen.

PowerKiDS press

New York

Published in 2014 by The Rosen Publishing Group, Inc.
29 East 21st Street, New York, NY 10010

Produced for Rosen by Ruby Tuesday Books Ltd
Editor for Ruby Tuesday Books Ltd: Mark J. Sachner
US Editor: Joshua Shadowens
Designers: Tammy West and Emma Randall

With special thanks to Steve Owen for his help in developing and making
the projects in this book.

Photo Credits:
Cover, 1, 4—5, 6—7, 8—9, 10—11, 12—13, 14—15, 16—17, 18—19, 20—21, 22—23,
24—25, 26—27, 28—29 © Ruby Tuesday Books and John Such; cover, 1, 3, 4—5,
6—7, 8—9, 10—11, 16, 22—23, 24 © Shutterstock.

Library of Congress Cataloging-in-Publication Data

Owen, Ruth, 1967—
 Ready, aim, fire! / Ruth Owen.
    pages cm — (DIY for boys)
 Includes index.
 ISBN 978-1-4777-6286-8 (library binding) — ISBN 978-1-4777-6287-5 (pbk.) —
 ISBN 978-1-4777-6288-2 (6-pack)
 1. Toy making—Juvenile literature. 2. Toy guns—Juvenile literature. 3.
Weapons—Juvenile liteature. I. Title.
 TT174.O94 2014
 745.592—dc23
                                  2013035232

Manufactured in the United States of America

CPSIA Compliance Information: Batch #W14PK8 For Further Information contact: Rosen Publishing, New York, New York at 1-800-237-9932

CONTENTS

WARNING!

Neither the author nor the publisher shall be liable for any bodily harm or damage to property that may happen as a result of carrying out the activities in this book.

READY, AIM, FIRE!

If you love target shooting, this is the book for you because you get to build your own rubber band gun, mini crossbow, and bow and arrow. NEVER aim these **devices** at people, animals, or property that could be damaged, though.

Why not try making some targets to shoot at? You can draw or paint paper targets, tape them to a piece of foam board, and then attach them to a fence. An old favorite is to build a shooting gallery out of empty metal cans or plastic bottles.

There's also two fun projects in the book that use paper balls and marshmallows as **ammunition**. Have fun firing these **missiles**, but never fire them at animals or items that might get damaged.

Rubber band gun

PAPER BALL SLINGSHOT

This first project uses everyday materials such as a wire coat hanger, duct tape, and rubber bands to make a small but powerful **slingshot**.

You can use the slingshot to shoot small folded-up pieces of paper or tiny crumpled-up balls of paper. If you really want to get mean, you can even soak the balls of paper in water and shoot disgusting soggy paper missiles at your friends.

Collect the materials you need, and in less than 30 minutes, you'll be ready to get aiming, firing, and splattering!

STEP 1:

Use the wire cutters to cut the coat hanger into two pieces, as shown.

STEP 2:

On the bottom part of the coat hanger, measure and then mark the center of the wire. Then add two more marks that are each half an inch (1.3 cm) from the center mark (marks A and B).

WARNING:

Only use wire cutters if an adult is there to help you.

Cut here

Cut here

Center mark

Mark A   Mark B

STEP 3:

Now bend the wire at marks A and B.

STEP 4:

To make the slingshot's handle, wrap the bent end of the wire with duct tape.

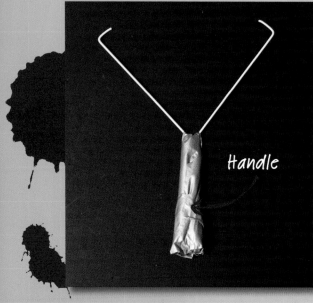

Handle

STEP 5:

Now bend the two top pieces of wire outward to make a Y shape.

STEP 6:

Bend the end of each top piece of wire to create a small loop.

STEP 7:

Loop the two rubber bands together, as shown, and then pull them tight.

STEP 8:

Hook the rubber bands into the small loops at the ends of the Y shape.

STEP 9:

Finally, wrap a small strip of duct tape around each of the loops to hold the rubber bands in place. The slingshot is now ready to be used. You can fire small folded-up pieces of paper or crumpled-up balls of paper.

READY, AIM, FIRE!

TRADITIONAL BOW AND ARROW

People have been using bows and arrows in warfare and for hunting for thousands of years. Different **cultures** around the world each developed their own versions of these weapons.

A bow is a **flexible** piece of wood that is made to bend, or flex, by a person pulling on a string that's attached to both ends of the bow. An arrow is held in the string, and as the string is released and the bow straightens, the arrow is propelled at high speed toward its target.

The sport of shooting with bows and arrows is called **archery**. In archery events at the Olympic games, competitors shoot, with incredible accuracy, at targets that are 230 feet (70 m) away!

Bows and arrows used in competitive archery are high-tech pieces of equipment.

String

Bow

Arrow

Traditional, homemade bow and arrow

YOU WILL NEED:

- A long piece of stripwood 1 inch (2.5 cm) wide with a curved profile (see additional notes below)
- A measuring tape
- A small saw or craft knife (for cutting the wood)
- Wood glue
- String
- A length of doweling
- A large pencil sharpener
- Approximately 6 inches (15 cm) of thin wire
- Duct tape
- A small piece of cardboard
- A black marker

WARNING:

Only use a saw or a craft knife if an adult is there to help you.

Bow

STEP 1:

To make your bow, you will need to cut the stripwood into one piece that's about three-quarters your height.

You will then need to cut a second piece that's half this length.

The wood should have a curved profile. This will make the bow feel more comfortable in your hand.

Curved profile

STEP 2:

Glue the shorter piece of wood to the middle of the bow.
The flat sides of each piece of wood should be glued together.

Glue the shorter piece of wood
to the center of the bow.

Glue the
flat sides
together.

When the two pieces of wood are joined, their curved profiles
create a smooth, rounded section in the center of the bow that
is easy and comfortable to hold.

STEP 3:

Using a saw or craft knife, cut two notches in each end
of the bow. These notches are for the string to tie around.

Notches

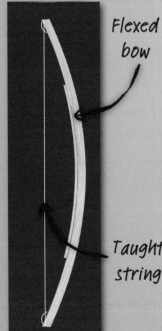

Flexed
bow

Taught
string

STEP 4:

Take a piece of string that's about
1 foot (30 cm) longer than the
bow. Loop and then tie one end
of the string around one end of
the bow so that the string sits
in the notches.

STEP 5:

Now tie the other end of the string
to the other end of the bow in the same way.
However, before you tie off this end, the string must
be pulled very taught. It should be so taught that the
bow starts to bend, or flex, as shown in the diagram.

STEP 6:
To make an arrow, measure and cut a piece of doweling so it's about 24 inches (61 cm) long.

STEP 7:
Use a large pencil sharpener to give one end of the doweling a sharp point, or tip.

STEP 8:
Wind some wire around the shaft of the arrow close to the tip. The wire will act as a weight and will help to stabilize the arrow as it flies. Wrap the wire in duct tape to hold the wire in place.

Wire

Tip of arrow

Wire secured with duct tape

STEP 9:
You can make the flights for your arrow using duct tape. Begin by cutting a 4-inch- (10-cm-) long piece of duct tape and lightly attaching it to the blunt end of the arrow's shaft.

STEP 10:

Cut a second piece of duct tape the same size and carefully stick it to one edge of the first piece.

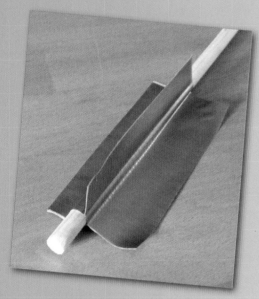

STEP 11:

Cut a third piece of duct tape, line up its long edges with the edges of the first and second pieces of tape, and then firmly press all three pieces of tape together around the arrow's shaft.

STEP 12:

To make sure that all three sections of the arrow's flights are exactly the same size and shape, draw and then cut out a cardboard template shape. Place the template onto one section of flat duct tape and draw around it.

Repeat on the other two sections of duct tape and then cut out the three shapes.

Duct tape flight

Cardboard flight template

STEP 13:

Wrap a narrow strip of duct tape above and below the flights to neaten and finish up the flights.

Notch

STEP 14:

Cut a small notch in the blunt end of the arrow.

STEP 15:

To fire the bow and arrow, hold the bow in one hand. With the other hand, position the arrow so the string sits in the notch at the end of the arrow. While holding the arrow, with the same hand pull back hard on the string so the arrow's tip protrudes just a few inches (cm) beyond the curve of the bow. Aim the arrow at your target, then let go of the arrow and string at the same moment.

If you've never tried firing a bow and arrow before, you may need some practice to perfect your technique. While this bow and arrow is a very simple design, it's a powerful device, however, that can be made to hit targets over 50 feet (15.2 m) away!

WARNING:

NEVER fire the bow and arrow at a person, an animal, or property that could be damaged.

MAKE A MINI CROSSBOW

People have been using crossbows for over 1,000 years. These devices shoot a long **projectile** called a bolt.

All you need to make this mini wooden crossbow are six pieces of wood, some wire, and rubber bands. Like the crossbows used in warfare for hundreds of years, this home-made crossbow is very powerful. It can easily shoot a wooden bolt over 50 feet (15 m).

Remember! The crossbow is designed to be used for target shooting only. Always be responsible when you are using the crossbow. Do not pull the string back until you are ready to shoot, and NEVER point the crossbow at a person, an animal, or property that could be damaged.

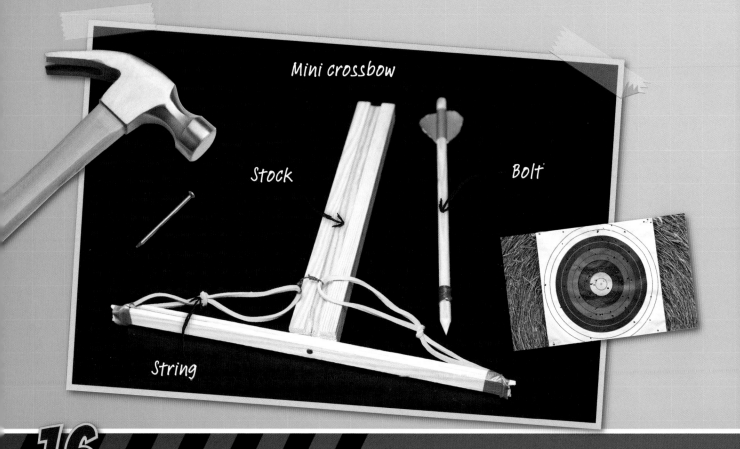

Mini crossbow

Stock

Bolt

String

YOU WILL NEED:

- A piece of wood 12 inches (30 cm) long, 1.5 inches (3.8 cm) wide, and 0.5 inches (1.5 cm) deep (this forms the stock of the crossbow)
- 4 pieces of stripwood 12 inches (30 cm) long, 0.5 inches (1.5 cm) wide, and 0.25 inches (0.6 cm) deep
- A piece of doweling 12 inches (30 cm) long with a diameter of 0.5 inches (1.5 cm)
- Wood glue
- A nail or tack
- A hammer
- A craft knife
- 2 long rubber bands (or four short ones)
- A piece of wire
- Duct tape
- A pencil sharpener
- A marker

WARNING:
Only use a craft knife and hammer if an adult is there to help you.

STEP 1:
Glue two pieces of the stripwood to the main piece of wood that forms the crossbow's stock.

Stripwood

Stripwood

Stock

Groove

The pieces of stripwood should be flush to the edges of the stock, leaving a 0.5-inch (1.5-cm) groove in the center for the crossbow's bolt to slide into.

STEP 2:
Take one of the remaining pieces of stripwood and using the craft knife, cut off 2 inches (5 cm) from one end.

STEP 3:

Place the shorter piece of stripwood and the remaining piece of stripwood against one end of the stock, so that the stock is central to the pieces of stripwood.

Glue and nail or tack the pieces of stripwood to the stock.

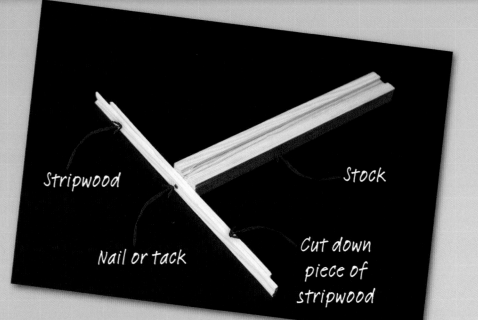

Stripwood

Stock

Nail or tack

Cut down piece of stripwood

STEP 4:

Cut a notch into each end of the longer piece of stripwood.

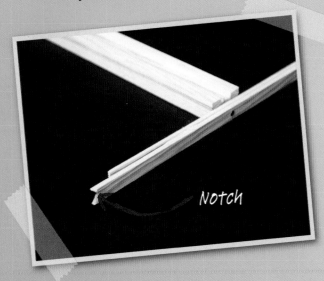

Notch

STEP 5:

To make the crossbow's string, take two long rubber bands, or knot two shorter bands together to make each side of the string.

Knot two rubber bands together as shown here. Then pull them tight.

STEP 6:

Join the two sides of the string together with some wire.

Wire

A long rubber band or two bands joined together

STEP 7:

To attach the string to the crossbow, hook one end of the string over one end of the stripwood.

Use duct tape to hold the string in place.

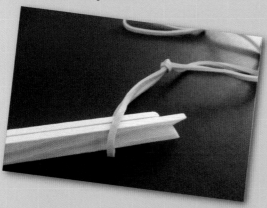

Hook the string through the notch. Then repeat at the other end of the stripwood with the other end of the string.

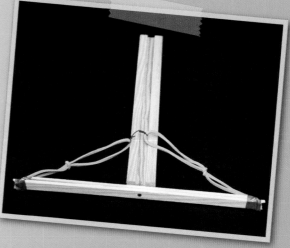

The crossbow is now complete.

STEP 8:

To make the bolt for the crossbow, sharpen one end of the piece of doweling using a large pencil sharpener.

STEP 9:

Make the bolt's flight, or tail, by taking a short length of duct tape and sticking it onto itself around the blunt end of the bolt.

STEP 10:

Draw a flight shape onto the duct tape, then cut out the flight.

Notch

STEP 11:

Cut a notch in the flight end of the bolt so it is lined up at the same angle to the flight, as shown.

STEP 12:

Wrap some wire around the bolt close to the pointed end. The wire will weigh down the pointed end of the bolt and stabilize it as it flies.

Once you start firing the crossbow, you can adjust the amount and position of the wire to achieve a more accurate shot.

Wire

STEP 13:

To prepare the crossbow for firing, slide the bolt into the groove in the stock. Slot the wire part of the string into the notch at the blunt end of the bolt.

To fire the crossbow, slide the bolt backward in the groove so the pointed end is level with the front of the stock and the string is pulled taught. Keep a tight grip on the blunt end of the bolt with your fingers until you are ready to take aim and release the bolt.

WARNING:

Remember: NEVER point the crossbow at a person or an animal.

Just like a traditional **peashooter**, this marshmallow gun uses puff power to fire marshmallows super-long distances. It's easy to put together because it's made from sections of water piping that you can buy from any plumbing supply store.

STEP 1:

Cut the water piping into the following lengths.

You won't need any glue to join the pieces of the marshmallow shooter because the T-piece and elbow joints are designed to tightly slot together with the water piping.

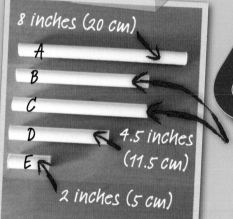

8 inches (20 cm)

A

B

C

D   4.5 inches (11.5 cm)

E

6 inches (15 cm)

2 inches (5 cm)

WARNING:

Only use a saw or pipe-cutting tool if an adult is there to help you.

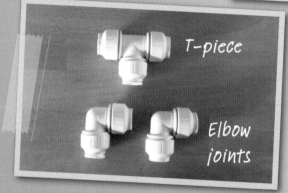

T-piece

Elbow joints

There are many different brands and designs of water piping, so the materials you buy don't have to look exactly like the ones in the pictures.

STEP 2:

Push pipe D into one end of an elbow joint.

Elbow joint

D

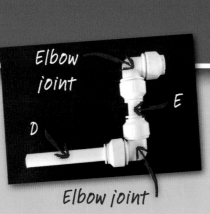

Elbow joint

D

E

Elbow joint

STEP 3:

Push pipe E into the other end of the elbow joint. Then push another elbow joint onto pipe E.

STEP 4:

Now push pipe B into the second elbow joint and add the T-piece to the other end of pipe B.

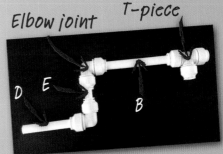

Elbow joint   T-piece

D   E

B

STEP 5:

Push pipe C into the bottom section of the T-piece to make a handle for the marshmallow shooter. Plug the end of the handle with some modeling clay.

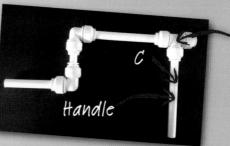

T-piece

C

Handle

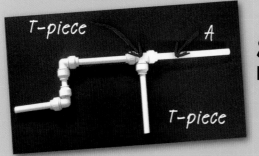

T-piece   A

T-piece

STEP 6:

Finally, push pipe A into the T-piece.

Blow here

Load a marshmallow into this end

STEP 7:

To load the marshmallow shooter, push a marshmallow into the end of pipe A and blow hard into pipe D. Have fun!

RUBBER BAND GUN

This easy-to-make, **retro** rubber band gun is created from small pieces of wood. It may look like a toy your grandfather would have played with, but it packs plenty of power.

Using rubber bands as its ammunition, this gun is a fun device to use for practicing your target shooting. For example, prop up playing cards in pairs on a wall and try to hit them. NEVER use the gun, however, to shoot at another person, an animal, or any piece of property that could be damaged.

STEP 1:
Cut the 1.5-inch- (3.8-cm-) wide stripwood into eight pieces. The pieces have been labeled with the letters of the alphabet.

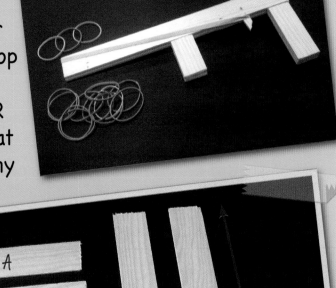

A

B

C

D

E

F

G

H

15 inches (38 cm)

6 inches (15 cm)

YOU WILL NEED:

- 6 feet (1.8 m) of stripwood that's 1.5 inches (3.8 cm) wide
- 12 inches (30 cm) of stripwood that's 0.5 inch (1.3 cm) wide
- A measuring tape
- A small saw
- A glue gun
- A pencil
- 2 wooden matches
- A wooden skewer
- A large, thick rubber band
- Smaller rubber bands for ammunition

STEP 2:

Glue piece A onto piece G at a right angle.

The top edge of piece A should be flush with the top edge of piece G.

STEP 3:

Glue piece B onto piece A, so the long edges of A and B are lined up.

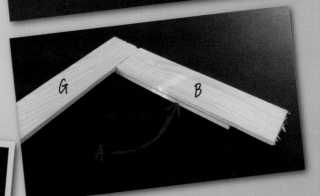

The top edge of piece C should be flush with the top edge of piece G.

This will be the gun's barrel

5 inches (13 cm)

STEP 4:

Glue piece C under piece G. The right-hand side of piece C should be 5 inches (13 cm) from the left-hand side of piece B.

STEP 5:
Glue piece D onto piece C, so the long edges of pieces C and D are lined up.

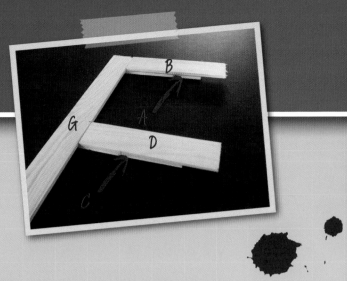

STEP 6:
Now, turn the gun over so that the barrel (piece G) is pointing to the right and pieces B and D are touching your work surface. Cut a 1.5-inch (3.8-cm) piece of the narrow stripwood. Then cut one end at an angle to create a point. Glue this piece of wood to the end of piece G, as shown.

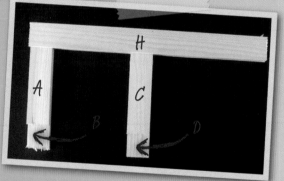

The point should protrude just over the top edge of piece G.

STEP 7:
Glue piece H onto the gun so that its edges are exactly even with piece G.

STEP 8:
Measure and mark a point on piece H that is 3 inches (7.6 cm) from the rear of the gun and 0.5 inch (1.3 cm) from the bottom edge of piece H.

STEP 9:
Now glue piece E to piece A, making sure the long edges of both pieces are lined up. Then, glue piece F to piece C. Again, make sure the long edges are lined up.

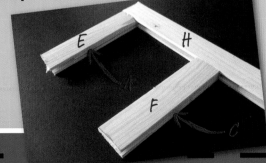

STEP 10:

Using the saw, now cut down the gun's two handles. Measuring from the bottom of the barrel, the rear handle should be 4 inches (10 cm) long, and the front handle should be 3 inches (7.6 cm) long.

E

H

F

4 inches
(10 cm) long

3 inches
(7.6 cm)
long

STEP 11:

Remove the ends of two matches, then glue the matches to the rear of the gun. You will look through the two matches, using them as a sight, when aiming the gun.

H

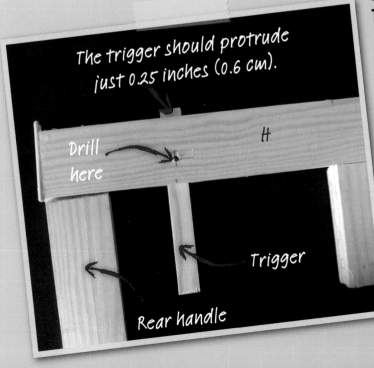

The trigger should protrude just 0.25 inches (0.6 cm).

Drill here

H

Trigger

Rear handle

STEP 12:

Take a piece of the narrow stripwood, approximately 4 inches (10 cm) long, and slide it between pieces G and H at the point you marked earlier, as shown. This piece is the gun's trigger.

STEP 13:

Drill all the way through piece H, the trigger, and piece G at the point you marked earlier. The hole should be small enough to be a tight fit for a wooden skewer.

STEP 14:

Push a short section of wooden skewer into the hole you drilled and out the other side. This will hold the trigger in the gun and allow it to move back and forth.

Trim down the trigger as required.

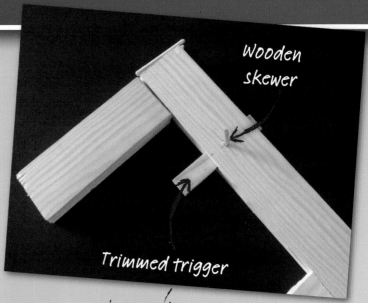

Wooden skewer

Trimmed trigger

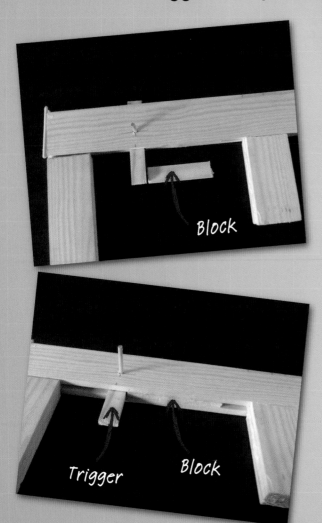

Block

Trigger   Block

STEP 15:

Now cut a piece of narrow stripwood to 2.5 inches (6.4 cm) long. This will be used as a block to keep the trigger from moving forward.

Slide the block between pieces H and G, and glue in place so it is a tight fit alongside the trigger.

STEP 16:

To neaten up the gun, snap off any pieces of skewer that are protruding out of the gun's barrel.

STEP 17:

Finally, stretch a large, thick rubber band from the front of the gun's barrel and around the trigger. When you squeeze the trigger, this rubber band pulls it back to its starting position.

Large, thick rubber band

Trigger

Front of barrel

STEP 18:

To load the gun with your rubber band ammunition, stretch a rubber band around the small point on the front of the barrel and around the small top section of the trigger. Take aim, then squeeze the trigger, and the rubber band will be fired at high speed!

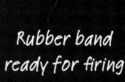

Point on barrel

Top of trigger

Rubber band ready for firing

WARNING:

NEVER fire the rubber band gun at a person, an animal, or property that could be damaged.

ammunition (am-yuh-NIH-shun)
Projectiles, such as bullets, arrows, and bolts, that are fired from weapons such as guns, bows, and crossbows.

archery (AR-chuh-ree)
The sport of shooting arrows from bows at targets.

cultures (KUL-churz)
Groups of people. The people of a particular culture live and express themselves in the same way through things such as language, dress, food, and celebrations.

devices (dih-VYS-ez)
Pieces of equipment that are designed for a particular purpose or to carry out a particular task.

flexible (FLEK-sih-bul)
Something that can be bent.

missiles (MIH-sulz)
Objects that are thrown or projected from weapons so that they hit other objects.

peashooter (PEE-shoot-ur)
A narrow tube that fires dried peas. A pea is loaded into one end of a peashooter then it is fired by the user blowing hard into the other end. Historically, peashooters were a popular toy for boys.

projectile (pruh-JEK-tyl)
An object that is thrown or projected from a weapon with great force.

retro (REH-troh)
Looking like something from the past.

slingshot (SLING-shot)
A small hand-held weapon that comprises a Y-shaped frame with a rubber string stretched between the two arms of the Y. A small missile is held in the string and when the string is stretched backward then let go, the missile is propelled forward at great speed.

WEBSITES
Due to the changing nature of Internet links, Powerkids Press has developed an online list of websites related to the subject of this book. This site is updated regularly. Please use this link to access the list:
www.powerkidslinks.com/dfb/fire/

Hardyman, Robyn. *Hunting.* Adventures in the Great Outdoors. New York: Windmill Books, 2013.

Howard, Melanie A. *Bowhunting for Kids.* Into the Great Outdoors. Mankato, MN: Capstone Press, 2013.

Shellhaas, Dave, and **Steve A. Shellaas.** *Outdoor Kids Club Ultimate Hunting Guide.* Greenville, Ohio: Miami Valley Outdoor Media, Ltd., 2011.

INDEX